United States
Department of
Agriculture

Forest Service

Southern
Research Station

General Technical
Report SRS–107

A Description and Comparison of Selected Forest Carbon Registries: A Guide for States Considering the Development of a Forest Carbon Registry

Jessica Call and Jennifer Hayes

I0410369

The Authors:

Jessica Call, Policy Analyst, U.S. Department of Agriculture Forest Service, Washington, DC; **Jennifer Hayes**, Management & Program Analyst, U.S. Department of Agriculture Forest Service, Rocky Mountain Research Station, Fort Collins, CO.

October 2007

Southern Research Station
200 W.T. Weaver Blvd.
Asheville, NC 28804

A Description and Comparison of Selected Forest Carbon Registries: A Guide for States Considering the Development of a Forest Carbon Registry

Jessica Call and Jennifer Hayes

Contents

A Description and Comparison of Selected Forest Carbon Registries: A Guide for States Considering the Development of a Forest Carbon Registry

Jessica Call and Jennifer Hayes

Abstract

There is increasing interest in tools for measuring and reducing emissions of carbon dioxide, a major greenhouse gas. Two tools that have been receiving a lot of attention are carbon markets and carbon registries. Carbon registries are established to record and track net carbon emission levels over time. These registries provide quantifiable and verifiable carbon for trade within a market. This report discusses the benefits and major elements of registries and then describes a selection of existing registries and protocols with forest carbon components. The report focuses on forests because of their carbon storage potential. The purpose of this report is to provide a starting point for any State government or other party considering the development of a carbon registry with a forestry component.

Keywords: Carbon, forest, markets, registry, sequestration.

Introduction

There is increasing interest in policy circles in possible tools for measuring and reducing emissions of carbon dioxide, a major greenhouse gas (GHG). Tools that have been receiving a lot of attention include carbon markets and carbon registries.

Carbon markets arise when entities interested in reducing carbon emissions purchase quantified reductions in carbon emissions and/or increases in carbon sequestration from other entities, often called carbon offsets. Forest carbon offsets reduce carbon levels in the atmosphere by increasing carbon storage in forest soils or biomass.

Carbon registries are established to record and track net carbon emission levels over time. Carbon registries have the potential to work in concert with carbon markets, helping to produce a quantifiable and verifiable carbon offsets for trade. Because forests have great carbon storage potential, efforts are underway in several regions to increase the use of forest carbon offsets and track forest carbon through registries.

The purpose of this report is to provide a starting point for any State government or other party considering the development of a carbon registry with a forestry component. In addition, even though the report is focused on carbon sequestration in forests, most of the concepts discussed also apply to carbon sequestration in other terrestrial ecosystems such as wetlands and grasslands.

The report discusses the benefits and major elements of registries and then describes a selection of existing registries and protocols with forest carbon components. A comparison table of existing registries is provided in appendix A. Information in appendix A and the remainder of this report was last updated on February 10, 2006. As many of the registries are still in development, significant changes may have occurred since the research for this report was completed in February of 2006. Please contact the individual registries for updated information. For readers unfamiliar with the basics of GHG emissions and sequestration, a brief background section on the key concepts of GHG reporting follows the "Introduction." A glossary of terms is provided in appendix B.

Background Concepts in Carbon Emissions and Sequestration

The term "greenhouse gas" refers to gases that trap heat in the Earth's atmosphere, namely carbon dioxide (CO_2), methane (CH_4), nitrous oxide (N_2O), hydrofluorocarbons, perfluorocarbons, and sulfur hexafluoride (SF_6) (Intergovernmental Panel on Climate Change 2001). Carbon dioxide is the GHG with the highest concentration in the atmosphere, and its atmospheric concentration has increased by around 30 percent since the preindustrial age (Intergovernmental Panel on Climate Change 2001). Although global GHG reduction efforts address all of the gases named above, this report deals only with carbon dioxide because of its central role in forest processes.

The concentration of carbon dioxide in the atmosphere is currently around 380 parts per million (Keeling and Whorf 2005). Atmospheric levels of carbon dioxide increase when the addition of carbon dioxide to the atmosphere (emission levels) is larger than the removal of carbon dioxide from the atmosphere. Humans contribute to carbon dioxide emission levels in a variety of ways including burning fossil fuels and deforestation. Removal of carbon dioxide from the atmosphere is often referred to as sequestration. Sequestration occurs naturally when plants absorb carbon dioxide and use it to grow, fixing carbon into biomass. It is also possible to sequester carbon through geological sequestration, in which carbon dioxide from the atmosphere is injected directly into underground geological formations (Intergovernmental Panel on Climate Change 2004). Terrestrial sequestration is the removal of carbon from the atmosphere by terrestrial ecosystems such as forests, grasslands, and wetlands. The systems that store the carbon, whether they are forests or caverns, are referred to as carbon sinks. Forests constitute a large carbon sink, and it is thought that net emissions of carbon dioxide to the atmosphere can be reduced by growing and preserving forests.

An organization seeking to reduce its carbon dioxide emissions levels may decide to fund emissions reduction or sequestration projects carried out by another party. The second party may be able to produce carbon savings at a lower cost, and the organization can, therefore, meet its emissions reduction targets more efficiently by purchasing the carbon savings, often called an offset, from the second party.

Carbon markets are created to facilitate the buying and selling of carbon offsets. A current barrier to the efficient functioning of carbon markets is that the quantification and verification of carbon offsets can be expensive. If the costs of conducting trades, known as transaction costs, are too high, then the incentives to produce, buy, and sell offsets will be reduced.

Why a Registry?

A registry can benefit landowners by providing a platform for documenting carbon sequestration on their land. In order to enter the emerging carbon market, landowners will need to quantify and verify how specific actions affect their carbon stocks.

A registry is a place where official records are kept. In the context of this report, forest carbon registries are places where entities can legally document their carbon emissions reduction efforts. A registry does not substitute for a market; rather it supplements the market by providing buyers with information about legally verifiable offsets. Registries have proliferated recently, internationally and nationally. While most of these registries are targeted at a broader range of GHG emissions, some registries specifically for forest carbon have been developed.

States may wish to develop registries with a forest carbon component for several reasons. The State may want to encourage and/or mandate reporting of carbon emissions and sequestration by companies and landowners in order to track emission and sequestration trends in the State. States may also want to use the registry to support the development of carbon markets in which registered carbon sequestration can become a tradable carbon credit. Registries can also be used to establish baseline levels of emissions against which future GHG reductions can be measured.

Major Registry Areas

Here, we describe the key components of registries. These are elements that all States need to consider when designing their forest carbon registries. While some examples of the registry elements are provided in the text, it may also be helpful to refer to the comparison of key elements of existing registries in appendix A.

In the context of a registry, governance is the legal basis for administration and management. It is the authority and the basis on which a registry is created, managed, and regulated. Several governance components need to be addressed in any registry. These include:

1. Defining the legal basis and purpose of the registry

2. Establishing administrative details for the registry

3. Defining the reporting entity for the registry

Legal Basis and Registry Purpose

First, the legal authority for the registry must be established. The legal authority can range from a legislative act to a voluntary agreement. Several State registries and the Federal 1605(b) program [Section 1605(b)] were created through legislative acts, with executive agencies then preparing the specific guidelines for the registries. Nongovernmental registries have also been established by both voluntary and legally binding agreements.

The legal basis for the registry often states the purpose of its existence. Diversity in registry purpose causes much of the confusion surrounding their development. A paper on registries by the Northeast States for Coordinated Air Use Management (NESCAUM) provides a helpful discussion on registry purposes, organizing registries into five tracks (Northeast States for Coordinated Air Use Management 2005). A single registry may develop one or more of the purpose tracks as they are not mutually exclusive. The five main purposes described by NESCAUM include:

1. To develop a State inventory of GHG emission and sequestration levels

2. To provide corporate and/or landowner GHG inventory assistance

3. To provide public recognition for entities taking action on climate change

4. To establish baseline protection, so that entities making emission reductions now won't be penalized under future regulatory schemes

5. To record emission reduction efforts and make them quantifiable and fungible, i.e., tradable in the market

An initial, key decision to make about the registry purpose and design is whether to make the registry voluntary or mandatory. This decision depends on the purpose of the registry and the State's goals. A State will probably want to make the registry mandatory if it wants to use the registry to collect accurate and consistent GHG data from a specific sector, or a variety of sectors; this data could then be used to establish a baseline for a GHG regulatory program. If the registry is intended solely for public recognition or to provide the private sector with GHG inventory assistance, then a voluntary registry will likely suffice. Appendix A tracks whether reporting is mandatory or voluntary for each of the included registries.

States may also want to use their registries to encourage particular forest management practices. These goals can vary considerably from State to State, with some States using registries to promote forest preservation and others using them to recognize active timber management.

Registry Administration

After establishing the legal basis and purpose of the registry, the State will need to decide who will actually run the registry. States may want an existing State agency to administer the registry, or they may wish to establish an independent group or designate a private entity to run the registry. California, for example, established a board of directors and staff for its Climate Action Registry that operates outside of other California State agencies (California Climate Action Registry 2006). Georgia, however, is developing its registry through the Georgia Forestry Commission (Georgia General Assembly 2004). States must also determine how the registry will be funded. Will the registry be created and maintained through State appropriated funds, will it charge a user fee, or will it use some other source of funding?

The State will also need to establish the registry infrastructure. At a minimum, there should be two parts to the infrastructure: (1) a database to house the registry information and (2) a reporting system, including guidelines to define entity and/or project boundaries. For example, will entities list their plots by latitude and longitude, georeferencing, or by land deed reference number? The registry will need to develop a basic reporting form that is consistent with the format of the registry and its database. The specific elements that will need to be reported to the registry are discussed throughout the remainder of this report.

Every registry must also determine who can report carbon emissions and offsets. Items for consideration include: whether to require a minimum number of acres for landowners to participate, whether to recognize landowner cooperatives, and whether to allow out-of-state entities to report. Finally, every registry must address how it will deal with the issue of enforcement. This is a major component of governance. Certification, one of the major ways to ensure and enforce that carbon registered is actually in existence, is discussed later in this report.

Definition of Reporting Entity

Another critical element of registry design is the definition of a reporting entity, i.e., what type and what level of an organization reports its activities to the registry. For most registries, the reporting entity is any distinct legal entity recognized under U.S. law, such as an individual landowner or a corporation. Certain registries may define an entity further. The California Forest Sector Protocols, for example, specify that an entity is "any individual, corporation or other legally constituted body, a city or county government agency that owns at least 100 acres of trees" (California Climate Action Registry 2006). Geographic and temporal boundaries are usually defined. For example, the registry may specify whether international actions can be reported, and for what time period reports may be filed.

Entity vs. Project Reporting

In discussing registry design, an important distinction is the difference between entity and project level reporting. For entity reporting, the recognized entity reports carbon emissions and sequestration for all activities under its jurisdiction. A timber company, for example, would report the emissions and sequestrations for all its timber lands, operations, and facilities. The entity may not show an overall reduction in emissions—the only obligation is to calculate and report its entire carbon budget.

Project level reporting deals with a planned activity, or set of activities, that removes, reduces, or prevents carbon emissions in the atmosphere. In this type of reporting a forest company might report a specific reforestation project that was designed to increase carbon storage. The focus would be on that specific project rather than the company's entire carbon budget.

In designing a registry, States will have to decide whether to support entity level reporting, project level reporting, or both. The decision will depend on the goals of the registry. If a registry is to create a State inventory of carbon emissions, then entity level reporting will be needed. If the State is more interested in tradable carbon offsets then project level reporting should be considered. Allowing for both types of reporting would create the most diverse and robust registry.

Ownership

Depending on the purpose and scope of the registry, States may want to consider the issue of carbon ownership. Carbon ownership is primarily an issue for States that want their registry to create and promote tradable carbon credits. If the sequestration projects listed in the registry are going to be traded in a carbon market then the registry can facilitate this process by establishing who retains the right to claim carbon ownership (at any given point in time) and which carbon pools are included in that ownership.

For example, who retains ownership rights if a third party is involved? Suppose a landowner has reforested 200 acres of land with trees donated by a local utility company. The State registry will need to establish who retains ownership rights to the carbon sequestered through the project—the landowner or the company that donated the trees. If the registry wants to recognize wood products as a carbon pool, then ownership issues can become even more complicated. If a landowner harvests his or her timber, a certain percentage of the tree carbon will remain sequestered in the harvested wood. When the wood is sold to a timber company, a State registry that recognizes this carbon pool will need to determine who retains ownership rights for the carbon—the original landowner or the timber buyer who now owns the wood.

A State may also decide that ownership issues are outside the scope of its registry. The California Registry, for example, considers ownership questions to be outside its realm of responsibility. If a State wants to promote the trading of carbon credits then it may need to establish guidelines for carbon ownership. This will be especially important for registries that recognize wood products as a carbon sink.

Liability

A registry's liability policy answers the question of who will be held responsible if a project or entity fails to sequester the carbon it initially said that it would. This relates back to the ability of a registry to enforce and ensure that carbon registered is actual carbon sequestered.

Miscalculations, changes in project design, and natural disturbances can cause the actual amount of carbon sequestered to be different from the original projection. Natural disturbances such as fire and storms are of particular concern when dealing with liability. If a reforested area burns in a wildfire, for example, a registry's liability policy will need to address who is responsible for making up the lost carbon and how the carbon "makeup" will occur.

There are two general approaches to liability in the marketplace—buyer liability and seller liability. In buyer liability, the purchaser of the carbon credit is responsible for any shortfall in the carbon sequestered by a project. In seller liability, the original landowner or project designer is responsible for any difference between the expected and actual carbon sequestration. Seller liability generally encourages heavy trading because more buyers enter the market since they bear no risk if the sequestration project fails. On the other hand, seller liability can be difficult to enforce, especially in a loose and emerging global carbon market. With buyer liability, the offset buyer will be responsible if the project fails, so the buyer is likely to buy only offsets that have little risk. The disadvantage of buyer liability is that it may discourage offset buyers from entering the market (Zhang 2001).

States could also develop an insurance program of sorts, to offset any shortfall in carbon levels that may occur. Policy groups have discussed the idea of using certified public or private lands as backup carbon storage, so that carbon stored in these reserves could be substituted for shortfalls in the registry projects. Another possibility is to have registry participants reserve a certain amount of their sequestration to make up for any carbon shortfalls. The Chicago Climate Exchange, for example, has its members reserve 20 percent of their sequestration or emission reductions to offset any shortfalls in their carbon emission reduction (Personal communication. 2005. Michael Walsh, Executive Vice President, and Murali Kanakasabai, Senior Econonist, Chicago Climate Exchange, 190 South La Salle St., Suite 1100, Chicago, IL 60603).

Quantification of Carbon

A central component of the registry is how to quantify an entity's carbon stocks and carbon sequestration activities. There are two basic components to this question: (1) what carbon will be quantified, and (2) what methods are accepted for the carbon measurement.

Types of forest carbon—It is helpful to group forest carbon into categories and carbon pools, as in the tabulation below, which was adapted from the California Forest Sector Protocol.

Category	Carbon pool
Living biomass	Tree biomass
	Shrubs and herbaceous understory
Onsite dead biomass	Standing dead biomass
	Lying dead wood
	Litter
Soil	Soil
Offsite	Wood products

A registry must establish which of these carbon pools entities are required to report and which pools are voluntary. The California Forest Project Protocol requires that living tree biomass, standing dead biomass, and lying dead wood be reported. The remaining pools—shrubs and herbaceous understory, litter, soil, and wood products—are voluntary and, therefore, not certified (California Climate Action Registry, www.climateregistry.org).

In deciding which carbon pools to make mandatory, important considerations include the quality and cost of the existing methods for measuring the carbon pool and the contribution of a carbon pool to the net change in forest carbon. For example, the measurement of soil carbon tends to be very costly and time intensive. While soil carbon is a large portion of a forest's overall carbon stock, the size of the pool often changes slowly and is difficult to measure over short timeframes. Because of this, many forestry registries have decided to make the reporting of soil carbon voluntary.

Measurement Methodology

Direct vs. Indirect Measurement

There are direct and indirect ways to measure forest carbon. Direct measurement involves sampling of the forested area, while indirect measurement relies either on models or carbon look-up tables that estimate the amount of carbon in a specific forest type of a certain age. Registry design must balance the need for data accuracy with the need for low transaction costs. If the costs for registry participation are too high, then the transaction costs for any associated carbon markets will discourage participation. If the measurement methods are too relaxed, then transaction costs may be low, but the data will not be credible enough to satisfy registry requirements or provide a basis for market transactions.

Direct sampling offers the best opportunity for accuracy, but is usually the most expensive and time intensive. Sampling methodology and sample plots must be established for the forest, measurements of the required carbon pools must be made within the sample plots, and methods must be developed to translate field measurements into carbon mass estimates for the entire forest area.

Models estimate the amount of carbon in a forest using factors such as timber volume, forest type, stand-size class, etc. The specificity of the model will depend on the detail of the inventory data that it receives. Models with local information such as tree sizes will provide more detailed output than models that only require general input such as forest type and stand-size class.

Carbon look-up tables provide standard estimates of forest carbon based on forest type, age, etc. The forest carbon data is generally the result of both forest carbon models and formal forest inventories. The look-up tables can be based on regional forest types or may be based on more locally specific information.

A registry needs to be clear about what types of carbon measurement methods it will accept. The California Registry, for example, requires direct sampling, while Section 1605(b) accepts a variety of look-up tables, models, and direct sampling options.

Accuracy

Designers of a registry will need to decide what level of accuracy it requires for carbon estimates. Most carbon models and look-up tables have an associated accuracy level; statistical confidence is typically used to assess the accuracy of direct sampling. The California Registry requires that the standard error of the carbon estimate be no > 20 percent of the mean carbon estimate (at a 90-percent confidence interval). The California Registry also applies a sliding scale of deductions for standard errors < 20 percent. For example, if the sampling error is between 5 and 10 percent of the mean estimate, then a 10-percent deduction is applied to the corresponding carbon pool (California Climate Action Registry 2006, Forest Protocols, June 2005, www.climateregistry.org/PROTOCOLS/FP).

In contrast, Section 1605(b) ranks estimation methods from level A to level D, with level A being the most accurate (U.S. Department of Energy 2005). For the forestry sector, level A estimates are from direct measurement using a sampling system designed to estimate changes in carbon stocks within 10 percent of the true value. Level B estimates typically use models to provide estimates within 20 percent of the true value, and level C estimates use look-up tables to provide estimates that are within 30 percent of the true value. Level D is more than 30 percent off the true estimate, so is considered to have inadequate accuracy. Where a combination of estimation methods are employed, a reporting entity's estimates must average at least level B accuracy to count as officially registered.

De Minimus Exclusions

Registries may allow entities to exclude a small amount of emissions from registry reporting, creating "de minimus exclusions." Typically this is done for the smaller emission components that are difficult to measure. An example could be a forestry company with a very small fleet of vehicles for employee use. If vehicle emissions are likely to account for a very small fraction of the company's overall emissions, then a registry may want to allow this emission source to be excluded from the company's report. This prevents entities from spending a large amount of resources measuring an emission source that has little impact on the entity's overall carbon budget.

Section 1605(b) allows up to 3 percent of an entity's emissions to be omitted from its reporting (U.S. Department of Energy 2005). The California Registry doesn't allow for any de minimus exclusions for required carbon stocks in either the entity or forest project protocols. [In effect, however, California does allow an exemption by making the reporting of soil and leaf litter carbon voluntary (California Climate Action Registry Forest Project Protocol, June 2005).] Most other registry programs have not addressed whether they will allow for de minimus exclusions; this is an issue they will need to address with their stakeholders.

Reporting

Registries must establish both a timeline and process for reporting. The timeline addresses how often an entity must report and the lag time between the reporting deadline and the time period covered by the report. Most registries to date require annual reporting. California requires that annual reports for emissions occurring in the previous calendar year be submitted by August 31 of the current year (California Climate Action Registry Forest Sector Protocol, June 2005); Section 1605(b) requires that the reports for the previous calendar year be submitted by July 1 of the current year (U.S. Department of Energy 2005).

Certification

A State will need to establish a process for certifying the quality and accuracy of the entity and/or project reports submitted to the registry. The most common approach is third-party certification, in which an independent, third party follows a set procedure for certifying each project or entity report submitted to the registry. The California Registry, for example, has an approved set of third-party certifiers and provides them with a standardized approach to follow in the certification process. In California, project and entity reporting must be certified every 5 years (California Climate Action Registry 2006, Forest Sector Protocol and Forest Project Protocol, June 2005).

If the registry has certification and/or inventory requirements, a reporting schedule will have to be developed for these as well. The California Forestry Sector Protocol requires third-party certification reports every 5 years, with a deadline of December 31 for a certification period that ends in the previous calendar year. California also requires that a forest inventory is completed every 10 years, so this would be an additional reporting requirement.

Not all registries require third-party certification. The U.S. Department of Energy (DOE) 1605(b) guidelines allow entities to self-certify their reports. However, registries with third-party certification are generally seen as providing more accurate and reliable information.

Forest Activities Accepted

It is important to define the types of forest activities that will be accepted into a State's registry. This decision might be based on the purpose of the registry, the prevalent forest activities in a given State, or the quality of the existing carbon measurement tools for that forestry practice. Afforestation and reforestation are the activities most commonly accepted by registries, primarily because they can be measured with the most certainty.

Effects of forest preservation and forest management activities on carbon pools are usually more difficult to measure. For forest preservation, the calculation of carbon gained depends on an accurate projection of what would have happened to the land without the preservation action. There has been considerable research on the carbon sequestration gains of various forest management activities, such as the research conducted for the Maine Climate Action Plan that estimates the carbon gains from various forest management practices (Personal communication. Rich Birdsey, 2005. Northern Global Change Program Manager, U.S. Department of Agriculture Forest Service, Northeast Area Research Station, 11 Campus Blvd. Suite 200, Newton Square, PA 19073. Personal communication. 2005. Kevin McDonald, Data Manager, Maine Department of Environmental Protection, 17 State House Station, Augusta, ME 04333). While we know more now that we did 10 years ago, there are still uncertainties and the amount of carbon stored is usually much less than in afforestation or reforestation projects.

In addition to the types of forest projects accepted, States must also decide whether to require registry activities to meet additional forest management standards. For example, several existing registries require that registered forest activities be conducted in accordance with State best management practices (BMP) or in a certified sustainable forest (California Climate Action Registry Forest Sector Protocol, June 2005) (Personal communication. 2005. Nathan McClure, Associate Chief Forester, Georgia Forestry Commission, 5645 Riggins Mill Rd., Dry Branch, GA 31020). States may also want to take a position on accepting nonnative trees. California, for example, only accepts native California forest types in its registry.

Baseline

In the context of carbon registries, a baseline is a point in time or a level of carbon from which an entity will measure changes in carbon stocks. There are many techniques for calculating baselines, but most of them can be described either as base-year methods or as moving baseline methods. In base-year methods a specific year (or span of several years) is selected for initial carbon measurement. Future measurements are then compared against this initial base-year measurement to determine the amount of carbon sequestered during the interval.

In moving baseline methods, one calculates a moving baseline that projects what the level of carbon would have been if the project were never undertaken. This projected baseline is then compared to the actual measured carbon to determine the change in carbon stocks due to the project. For project reporting, the moving baseline approach is better than the base-year approach at addressing the question of additionality, i.e., the additional amount of carbon sequestered that would not have been sequestered had the activity not taken place.

Additionality

Additionality addresses the question of whether the carbon storage produced by a project is actually additional to what would have occurred had the project not taken place. If a registry is to record projects that create a quantifiable and fungible carbon offset, then it will need to address additionality requirements. The true sequestration gain of the project cannot be known unless the registry also looks at what level of sequestration would have taken place in the absence of the project.

For example, imagine a project that reforests 500 acres of land where a timber harvest recently took place. This reforestation project would report its carbon gains against a baseline level of carbon storage. Imagine that the State where the project occurs has established a single year baseline for reforestation projects, in which the base year is 1-year postharvest. Under this baseline approach, the carbon storage generated by the project would be all of the carbon present in the system at the end of the project term minus the amount of carbon that was present 1-year post timber harvest. However, the State law where this project occurs requires that all timber harvests be replanted to produce a certain basal area in 25 years. The level of forest carbon generated through this State requirement then becomes the expected base carbon stock (the expected basal-area stocking level in 25 years). All of

the carbon stored since 1-year postharvest is therefore not truly "additional." By State law, the landowner would have had to replant the land anyway, so the legally required basal area would have been present without the carbon project. The reforestation project will report different levels of carbon storage depending on the additionality requirements it follows. The carbon gains of the project will be much smaller if the landowner only counts as additional any carbon gains that exceed the State's basal-area requirement.

The idea of additionality is contentious and has been addressed differently by most States. For this reason, this is one area that could lead to future debate between States, regarding what additionality provisions should be required. California only counts as additional any forest projects that go above and beyond State forestry requirements, whereas the entity reporting required by Section 1605(b) has no specific requirements to prove additionality. If an entity using Section 1605(b) counted all carbon growth from a base year as additional, then a carbon offset in California would not be equivalent to the carbon offset under Section 1605(b) because they would have different reference points.

Permanence

Permanence refers to the ability to ensure that carbon will be sequestered for an agreed upon time period. Entities registering forest carbon can work towards permanence by utilizing long-term conservation easements. This method is required by California in its forest carbon protocols. The easement allows the landowner to practice forestry, but ensures that the overall landscape is protected and will retain carbon for a designated time period. It may be better to consider certain forest carbon credits temporary rather than permanent. Registries could offer shorter contract times for shorter term forest projects, where carbon credits were guaranteed on a 10- or 20-year basis. Permanence is an especially important issue for registries that are intended to promote marketable offsets—offset buyers will want to know the duration of the carbon storage they have purchased.

Leakage

Leakage is the shifting of activities from inside a carbon offset project's boundaries to outside the offset project's boundaries. This shift results in an increase in carbon emissions outside the project's physical boundaries. There are two types of leakage: (1) activity-shifting leakage and (2) market leakage. Activity-shifting leakage occurs when an activity is simply shifted from one area of a company's property to another. For example, if a landowner conserves forestland on one part of his or her property as an offset project, but relocates the timber harvest to another section of his or her land as a result, then leakage occurs. When there is leakage, the actual carbon sequestration will be the sequestration by the official project minus the emissions from the leakage activity. The California Forest Project Protocols require that reporting entities account for activity-shifting leakage (California Climate Action Registry Forest Project Protocol, June 2005).

Market leakage occurs when a carbon offset project causes a change in activity outside of the reporting entity's boundaries through shifts in market demand and supply. For example, if timber harvesting is reduced on one landowner's land in a region, then demand may simply shift to another landowner in the region, resulting in no net increase in carbon sequestration for the region (Sampson and Grover 2005). Market leakage is very difficult to measure and such measurement is not currently required by existing State registries.

Overview of Existing Registries

The spreadsheet in appendix A provides a comparison of existing carbon registries for the forestry sector, focusing on the most developed U.S. State programs (including the Oregon affiliated nonprofit Climate Trust), the U.S. Federal registry [1605(b)], and two different carbon markets—the Chicago Climate Exchange and the market for Clean Development Mechanisms (CDM) established by the Kyoto Protocol. The spreadsheet also summarizes the recently issued GHG project protocols that were developed by the World Resources Institute (WRI) and World Business Council for Sustainable Development (WBCSD). The WRI/WBCSD Project Protocol is an addition to the original WRI/WBCSD GHG Protocol, which many consider to be the international standard for GHG emission reporting.

The Land Use, Land-Use Change and Forestry (LULUCF) good practice guidance issued by the Intergovernmental Panel on Climate Change (IPCC) is another set of reporting standards that are frequently referred to in the GHG literature. The LULUCF guidance includes broader based guidelines for multiple land use sectors (cropland, grassland, forestland, etc.) and is, therefore, better suited to large-scale inventories than specific registries. The LULUCF guidance is still included in the spreadsheet comparison, however, to provide additional background information on carbon reporting techniques.

Each spreadsheet column refers to a specific registry and each row refers to a registry element to be compared across registries. For better organization registry elements are grouped into major registry areas discussed previously in this report, including:

1. Governance
2. Ownership
3. Liability
4. Types of forest carbon
5. Measurement methodology
6. Reporting
7. Certification
8. Forest activities accepted
9. Baseline and additionality
10. Permanence
11. Leakage

The descriptions of these registry elements provide a detailed comparison of the major carbon registries with a forestry element. A more general description of each major registry is provided below. Note that not all of the programs described follow a conventional registry format. Each program, however, contains common registry elements that provide examples to States considering the development of their own registry or carbon offset programs.

U.S. Department of Energy 1605(b) Guidelines

Section 1605(b) of the 1992 Energy Policy Act required the Department of Energy (DOE) to create a national registry for the voluntary reporting of GHG emissions. DOE issued guidelines for Section 1605(b) in 1994, and these are the guidelines currently in use by reporting entities. DOE issued revised guidelines for public comment in the spring of 2005 and is currently reviewing public comments and making needed changes to the revised guidelines. Reporting entities will continue to use the 1994 guidelines until the final, revised guidelines are issued. This report discusses the interim revised guidelines that were issued in the spring of 2005.

Section 1605(b) is organized around entity reporting, in which an entity is a "distinct entity under US, state or local law." Under this system, businesses report the net GHG emissions for their organization as a whole instead of reporting individual sequestration or emission activities separately. Section 1605(b) does not actually prohibit project level reporting, but it lacks the project-specific guidelines found in most registries with project level reporting. Section 1605(b) accepts a variety of GHG measurement and accounting techniques and does not require third-party certification. For further detail on Section 1605(b) please refer to the comparison matrix in appendix A.

California Climate Action Registry

The California Climate Action Registry was created through California SB1771 and SB527, and was signed into law in 2001. The enabling legislation establishes the California Registry as a voluntary registry, but also states that the purpose of the registry is to establish a baseline for emissions against which any future GHG regulations may be applied. Along these lines, California also guarantees its "best efforts" to ensure that registry participants' early actions are considered in the event of any future State, Federal, or international regulatory scheme.

The California Registry has established a general protocol for all registry participants and industry specific protocols that include a forestry sector protocol and a forestry project protocol. The forestry sector protocol deals with entity level reporting, in which an entity is "an individual, corporation or other legally constituted body, a city or county government agency that owns at least 100 acres of trees." The forestry project protocol describes the requirements for project reporting, in which a project is a planned set of activities to reduce carbon dioxide emissions through carbon sequestration in forests. As a whole, the California Registry has much stricter requirements than Section 1605(b), especially for project level reporting. The forestry sector and forestry project protocols are described separately in appendix A.

Georgia Carbon Sequestration Registry

Georgia SB356 of 2004 requires the Georgia Forestry Commission to create the Georgia Carbon Sequestration Registry. The stated purpose of the Georgia Registry is to encourage voluntary actions to reduce GHG emissions and to ensure that sources in the State receive proper recognition for certified sequestration efforts under any future Federal or international regulation scheme.

Unlike Section 1605(b) and the California Registry, the Georgia Registry is intended solely for terrestrial carbon sequestration projects. Many of the specifics of the registry are still in development, but a few provisions have been established. The Georgia Registry will be an automated registry that accepts electronic submissions, ownership of the carbon will not be tied permanently to the land, and forests registered must contain native Georgia trees and be managed in accordance with Georgia's Forestry BMPs. Further information is provided in appendix A.

Maine Climate Action Plan

Maine Public Law 237, passed in 2003, instructs the Maine Department of Environmental Protection to create a Climate Action Plan for the State. The Climate Action Plan created calls for the creation of a statewide GHG registry and proposes measures to cut Maine's GHG emissions to 10 percent below 1990 levels by 2020.

Efforts to create a Maine GHG registry have merged with efforts to create the Regional Greenhouse Gas Registry (RGGR) for the Northeast. The RGGR is currently in development and should be completed in 2006. The plan is that the RGGR will not contain any specific guidelines for the forestry sector. Instead, the RGGR is to defer to the development of offset protocols by the Regional Greenhouse Gas Initiative, a cooperative agreement by Northeastern and Mid-Atlantic States to reduce GHG emissions. Concurrently, the Forest Service, U.S. Department of Agriculture has awarded a grant to the Pinchot Institute to work with Maine, Pennsylvania, and Wisconsin to develop regional protocols, with the intention that these protocols will be applied to State and regional registries in the Northeast.

Since RGGR and the Pinchot Institute's work are still underway, the comparison matrix in appendix A contains fewer specifics on the Maine registry. However, there has been significant research in Maine on the potential to increase carbon storage through the use of wood products, alternative timber management practices, and the use of woody biomass for fuel. It is, therefore, likely that any future Maine registry will allow these practices to be registered as part of an entity's carbon budget. The efforts in Maine and at RGGR also provide a good example of how State registry efforts can work and potentially merge with regional registries.

Oregon Forestry Carbon Offsets

Oregon HB2200 (2001) authorized the Oregon State Forester to aggregate and market carbon offsets from forestry projects on State and private land and called for the creation of an accounting system to calculate and certify the carbon offsets created by the forestry projects. While this doesn't create a conventional carbon registry for Oregon, it does ask the department of forestry to create an offset accounting system that would contain many of the same elements present in registries.

The development of the accounting system and the process for aggregating and marketing forestry projects is more or less on hold in Oregon as of fall 2005. The Oregon Department of Forestry has found little demand for carbon offsets from forestry projects, so it is waiting until demand for the offset project increases to proceed further with the process.

The Climate Trust

The Climate Trust is a nonprofit organization whose mission is to provide GHG offset projects and to advance sound offset policy. Offset projects are designed to meet or exceed evolving international standards. The Climate Trust does not operate a registry per se, but it does have protocols for measuring and certifying offset projects and these protocols include many of the same elements found in registries.

Interested parties can purchase certified carbon offsets from the Climate Trust to meet their own carbon reduction needs. For example, new Oregon utilities are required to offset their GHG emission by 17 percent. Many companies are doing this by purchasing offsets from the Climate Trust. The Climate Trust operates by issuing Requests for Proposals for sequestration projects, and then evaluating project proposals based on their calculation and reporting schemes, likelihood of success, and other factors. The projects are, therefore, funded before the actual sequestration takes place, and the project leader uses the funding to implement and verify the proposed forestry project. The carbon purchase agreement defines carbon ownership rights, performance evaluation, and additional monitoring details that are part of an ongoing project management plan. In order to diversify its carbon portfolio, Climate Trust is limiting forestry projects to 25 percent of its future offset projects. Further information on the Climate Trust is provided in appendix A.

Chicago Climate Exchange

The Chicago Climate Exchange (CCX) is a voluntary, pilot GHG cap-and-trade program through which participants make voluntary and legally binding agreements to reduce emission to 4 percent below 1998 to 2001 levels by 2010. (Under the rules for CCX phase II, all CCX members must make a legally binding commitment to achieve entity-wide emission reductions of 6 percent below baseline by the end of 2010.) The infrastructure for the trading program essentially functions as a registry with the additional component of carbon credit trading. CCX members include commercial forestry companies, and CCX has developed protocols for the forestry companies to quantify and report their carbon stocks. CCX also permits the use of forestry projects as exchange offsets. Through exchange offsets, forest carbon sequestration projects become verified carbon credits that can be traded among CCX members. Please refer to appendix A for further details on CCX commercial

forestry sector protocols and the protocols for CCX exchange offsets.

Kyoto Protocol Clean Development Mechanism

The Kyoto Protocol authorizes annex 1 countries (developed nations) to offset 1 percent of their emissions through sequestration activities via CDMs. CDMs are carbon offset projects in developing countries and can range from renewable energy projects to reforestation. Developed nations may wish to fund CDMs because the costs of the offset projects may be less than the cost of emission reductions within the developed nation's own boundaries.

Afforestation and reforestation are the only forestry projects recognized through the CDM. CDMs must be validated and verified by a third party and ultimately approved by the CDM Executive Board. This process has proved lengthy and complex, and as of November 2005 no forestry projects have been approved by the CDM Executive Board. Further details on CDMs are found in appendix A.

World Resources Institute and World Business Council for Sustainable Development Project Protocol

WRI/WBCSD issued the GHG Protocol for Project Accounting (Project Protocol) in December 2005. The Project Protocol is a part of the Greenhouse Gas Protocol Initiative, a multistakeholder partnership of businesses, nongovernmental organizations, governments, and academics convened by WRI/WBCSD to develop internationally accepted GHG accounting and reporting standards. The Project Protocol is the second module developed by the GHG initiative; the first module was the GHG Protocol Corporate Accounting and Reporting Standard, which is generally accepted as the international standard for GHG reporting.

The Project Protocol provides principles and methods for quantifying and reporting GHG reductions from projects that reduce GHG emissions, increase the storage of carbon, or increase GHG removals from the atmosphere. The purpose of the Project Protocol is to provide a credible and transparent approach for quantifying GHG reductions in order to enhance the credibility of project reporting and promote harmonization among existing project-based GHG initiatives and programs.

The Project Protocol is a general protocol that is applicable to all economic sectors. Protocols with specific instructions for the land use sector are slated for issue sometime in 2006.

Intergovernmental Panel on Climate Change and Land Use, Land-Use Change and Forestry Good Practice Guidance

The IPCC, established by the World Meteorological Organization and the United Nations Environment Program, has issued guidelines on calculating national GHG inventories. The recommendations for the forestry sector are included in the 2003 report entitled "Good Practice Guidance for Land Use, Land Use Change and Forestry." The LULUCF guidance is targeted at the development of national GHG inventories, which examine GHG emissions on a much broader scale than GHG registries do. The LULUCF guidance, therefore, does not provide all the information needed for development of a carbon registry. It does, however, provide general principles and methods for GHG accounting that should also be helpful in registry development.

Conclusions

While each forest carbon program discussed in this report includes a registry in some shape or form, the goals of the registries vary significantly. These differences in purpose, along with other factors, contribute to the variation seen across other registry elements. The most significant differences are in the following areas:

- **Baseline and additionality:** Registries such as the California Forestry Project Protocol and the Kyoto Protocol's CDM take a strict approach to additionality, in which projects must prove that the carbon sequestered would not have been sequestered without the project in question. This requires the use of a moving baseline that projects how much carbon would have been sequestered in the absence of the project, given current conservation trends, forestry regulations, etc. The other approach, from the entity rather than a project perspective, is to use the carbon stocks from a starting year (or average of years) as the baseline and to account any increase in carbon stocks from the base year as additional carbon stored. This is the approach specified by Section 1605(b). For a single project, the amount of stored carbon calculated with a moving baseline will not be the same as the amount of stored carbon calculated with a fixed baseline, and this difference gives rise to product compatibility issues within emerging carbon markets.

- **Forest activities accepted:** Registries vary in the types of forest activities they recognize, with the primary difference being the types of forest management practices allowed. At one end of the spectrum is the Kyoto

Protocol's CDM, which only recognizes reforestation and afforestation projects. States such as Maine and Georgia plan to allow working timberlands in their registry and are considering including wood products as a recognized carbon pool in their registries. If wood products are included, then a carbon offset registered with Georgia or Maine would not meet the criteria for a CDM offset, creating nonequivalent offsets in the marketplace. The methodologies for projects such as forest biofuel use and reduction of forest fire risk require more research and development at this point, but may be included in a registry in the future.

- **Permanence:** Permanence requirements of existing registries differ. For example, the California Registry requires a permanent forest easement, while Section 1605(b) has no such requirement and simply measures carbon stocks from year to year. These differences would not necessarily make the products of the registries incompatible, but there would need to be a system to differentiate carbon credits based on the storage period of the carbon.

- **Certification requirements:** The primary difference here is whether a registry requires third-party certification or allows self-certification. Most registries require third-party certification, although the specific certification standards may vary. Section 1605(b) is the major exception—entities can certify their own reports. The rigor and consistency of a certification scheme are important to ensuring confidence in a registry and the carbon credits it may produce.

Differences between registries can also be seen as either nuts and bolts differences in accounting and methodology or as differences in the forest policies that governments and organizations want to advance with their registries. The challenge is to create registries with enough common elements to promote national level carbon credit trading with manageable transaction costs while still allowing States the flexibility needed to advance their own particular forest policy goals.

A difficulty for all registries will be the balance between data credibility and data costs. Credibility requires high-quality data, but high-quality data is expensive. If the data requirements are too stringent, then the transaction costs of the registry may prevent significant participation. States will need to assess the particular data needs of their registries to design data requirements that create trustworthy data without discouraging registry participation.

References

California Climate Action Registry. 2006. About us. http://www.climateregistry.org/ABOUTUS/. [Date accessed: February 16, 2006].

California Climate Action Registry. Forest project protocol. http://www.climateregistry.org/PROTOCOLS/. [Date accessed: June 2005].

California Climate Action Registry. Forest sector protocol. http://www.climateregistry.org/PROTOCOLS/. [Date accessed: June 2005].

Climate Trust. 2005. Request for carbon offsets. http://www.climatetrust.org/solicitations_2005_RFP.php. [Date accessed: November 2005].

CO2e.com. Homepage. http://www.co2e.com/common/faq.asp?intPageElementID=30136&intCategoryID=93. [Date accessed: November 2005].

Georgia General Assembly. 2004. Georgia Carbon Sequestration Registry Act (SB 356). http://www.legis.state.ga.us/legis/2003_04/sum/sb356 htm. [Date accessed: December 2005].

Intergovernmental Panel on Climate Change. 2001. Climate change 2001: the scientific basis. Cambridge University Press. http://www.grida no/climate/ipcc_tar/ [Date accessed: August 2005.]

Intergovernmental Panel on Climate Change. 2004. IPCC special report on carbon dioxide "Capture and Storage." http://arch rivm nl/env/int/ipcc/pages_media/SRCCS-final/IPCCSpecialReportonCarbondioxideCaptureandStorage.htm. [Date accessed: August 2005].

Keeling, C.D.; Whorf, T.P. 2005. Atmospheric CO_2 records from sites in the SIO air sampling network. In: Trends: a compendium of data on global change. Oak Ridge, TN: U.S. Department of Energy, Oak Ridge National Laboratory, Carbon Dioxide Information Analysis Center.

Maine Department of Environmental Protection. 2004. Maine climate action plan. http://maineghg raabassociates.org/finalplan.asp. [Date accessed: August 2005].

Northeast States for Coordinated Air Use Management. 2005. Draft State GHG registry emissions information programs issue paper. http://www.rggr.us/documents html and http://www.easternclimateregistry.org//registriesbackground html (summary). [Date accessed: December 2005].

Oregon General Assembly. 2001. HB 2200. Relating to forest carbon offsets. http://www.leg.state.or.us/01reg/measures/hb2200.dir/hb2200.en html. [Date accessed: August 2005].

Pew Center on Climate Change. 2005. Global warming basics. http://www.pewclimate.org/global-warming-basics/. [Date accessed: December 2005].

Sampson, R.N.; Grover, M. 2005. Carbon sequestration: a handbook. National Carbon Offset Coalition and The Sampson Group, Inc. 305 W. Mercury, Room 408, Butte, MT 59701. http://ncoc.us. [Date accessed: February 2006].

United Nationals Framework Convention on Climate Change. Clean Development Mechanism homepage. http://cdm.unfccc.int/. [Date accessed: December 2005].

U.S. Department of Energy. 2005. Section 1605(b) of the Energy Policy Act of 1992: guidelines for voluntary greenhouse gas reporting. http://www.pi.energy.gov/enhancingGHGregistry/generalguidelines html. [Date accessed: December 2005].

U.S. Environmental Protection Agency. Homepage. http://www.epa.gov/sequestration/baselines.html. [Date accessed: August 2005].

World Resources Institute/World Business Council for Sustainable Development. 2005. GHG protocol for project accounting. http://www.ghgprotocol.org/. [Date accessed: December 2005].

Zhang, ZhongXiang. 2001. The liability rules under international GHG emissions trading. Energy Policy. 29(7): 501-508.

Appendices

Appendix A
Comparison of Carbon Registries, Forestry Sector

Program	Federal 1605(b) program	California Forestry Sector Protocol, entity reporting	California Forestry Project Protocol, project certification
	Governance		
Web site	http://www.pi.energy.gov/ enhancingGHGregistry/ generalguidelines.html	http://www.climateregistry.org/ PROTOCOLS/	http://www.climateregistry.org/ PROTOCOLS/
Legal basis	The basis is a Federal law, Section 1605(b) of the Energy Policy Act of 1992. The DOE administers the program.	The basis is California laws SB1771 (2000) and SB812 (2002). The California Registry Board administers this voluntary GHG registry.	The basis is California laws SB1771 (2000) and SB812 (2002). The California Registry Board administers this voluntary GHG registry.
Purpose	The program is a voluntary GHG registry. Anyone can report any activities to the registry that they like. Reports are not registered unless they meet certain quality assurance standards.	The program is a voluntary GHG registry. It accepts all GHG emissions data, both biological and nonbiological, e.g., emissions data for electricity use in forestry practices.	The program provides certification of GHG emission reductions. It is meant to provide for transparent, credible, and consistent accounting of GHG reductions in the forestry sector.
Current status	Final draft guidelines that incorporate the latest round of public comments are under revision by DOE.	The program is up and running.	The program is up and running.
Voluntary or required	Voluntary	Voluntary	Voluntary
Registry management/ State agency responsibilities	The program is administered by the DOE.	The program is administered by California Climate Action Registry, an entity created by the State government to manage the registry. The program uses an online reporting system (CARROT).	The program is administered by California Climate Action Registry, an entity created by the State government to manage the registry. The program uses an online reporting system (CARROT).
Definition of reporting entity	A reporting entity must be a "distinct entity under US, state or local Law." The reporting entity is expected to be the entity with financial control of the forest.	The reporting entity is an "individual, corporation or other legally constituted body, a city or county government agency that owns at least 100 acres of trees."	The program deals with forest projects and not with entities. A forest project is a planned set of activities to remove, reduce, or prevent CO_2 emissions through carbon sequestration in forests. The project may apply to be a geographic subset of forest controlled by an entity or the entire forest area.
Forestry cooperatives recognized	Not specified	The program does not recognize forest cooperatives as entities.	The program does not recognize forest cooperatives as entities.
Future regulatory promises	None	California promises that registrants will receive consideration in any future GHG regulatory program.	California promises that registrants will receive consideration in any future GHG regulatory program.

continued

Program	Federal 1605(b) program	California Forestry Sector Protocol, entity reporting	California Forestry Project Protocol, project certification
Compatibility with other carbon programs	At this point 1605(b) requirements alone would not be enough for acceptance by the California Registry, CCX, or the Kyoto Protocol's CDM.	An entity registered with the California Registry would be qualified for registry with 1605(b) and CCX. The Kyoto CDM deals with projects, not entities. Requirements of other State registries now under development are unlikely to be stricter than those of the California Registry.	A forestry project that would meet California's registry requirements would also meet the requirements of 1605(b) and the CCX. CDM projects must be in developing countries. Other State registries now under development will likely have less strict requirements than the California Forestry Project Protocols.
National and international emissions	International reductions can be registered, but they must be in addition to and separate from domestic emissions.	National reporting is optional. Only California emissions are certifiable; international emissions and reductions are not accepted.	Forest projects must be in California.
		Ownership	
Ownership of carbon vs. land ownership	The program does not specify ownership, but the landowner always gets the reporting credit, even if a third party was involved.	The owner of the trees has the reporting responsibility. The program does not deal directly with the question of carbon ownership vs. land ownership.	The owner of the trees has the reporting responsibility. The program does not deal directly with the question of carbon ownership vs. land ownership.
Ownership of dead carbon	Not specified	NA (see above)	NA (see above)
Ownership of live carbon	Not specified	NA (see above)	NA (see above)
		Liability	
Liability (who is responsible if project fails to sequester carbon)	The program does not address this issue.	The owner of the trees is responsible for accounting/reporting change in carbon stocks.	The owner of the trees is responsible for accounting/reporting change in carbon stocks.
Natural disturbance	Emissions resulting from natural disturbance are not required to be reported, but if not reported, any regrowth resulting from disturbance will not count toward sequestration registered.	The baseline must be updated if natural disturbance has a cumulative effect of more than a 10-percent change in carbon stocks.	If a significant natural disturbance or unplanned harvest occurs (one that affects at least 20 percent of the project total carbon stock), then the affected area must be directly sampled within 3 years.
		Types of Forest Carbon	
Carbon pools required	The program does not specify this but recommends the inclusion of living tree biomass always and soil for reforestation efforts.	The program specifies that living tree biomass, standing dead biomass, and lying deadwood pools are to be included.	The program specifies that living tree biomass, standing dead biomass, and lying deadwood pools are to be included.

continued

Program	Federal 1605(b) program	California Forestry Sector Protocol, entity reporting	California Forestry Project Protocol, project certification
Carbon pools voluntary	Herbaceous vegetation, litter, deadwood, and wood products are recommended to optional, depending on the type of forestry activity.	Shrubs and herbaceous understory, litter, soil, and wood products may be included.	Shrubs and herbaceous understory, litter, soil, and wood products may be included.
Offsite carbon			
Wood products	Wood products are recognized as a carbon sink.	Reporting of wood products is optional. If wood products are reported, this does not confer ownership (as this is considered beyond the scope of the registry). There is a weight deduction for mill inefficiencies (keep 60 percent). The harvested wood pool is reported on a declining scale until it is discounted to zero.	Reporting of wood products is optional. If reported, the wood products component is not currently certified. There is a weight deduction for mill inefficiencies (keep 60 percent). The harvested wood pool is reported on a declining scale until it is discounted to zero.
Biomass energy	Biofuels are considered separately in the nonforest emissions sector of the registry.	Biofuels are accounted for in general energy use protocols.	Tree removal for biomass energy is not currently considered in the FPP.
	Measurement Methodology		
Calculation/ estimation methods (or metrics and data protocols)	A stock change accounting approach is employed. Certain estimation models such as COLE are approved for use.	A stock change accounting approach is employed. Example allometric equations are provided but others may be certified. Certain empirically based models are accepted where direct sampling is not required in off years.	Same as for forest sector protocol.
Sampling and/or monitoring methods	No specific sampling methods are required.	A sampling methodology is required; list of minimum required sampling criteria found in table 1.1 of forestry sector protocol.	A sampling methodology is required; list of minimum required sampling criteria found in table 1.1 of forestry sector protocol.
Accuracy/quality control standards	Estimation methods are rated A to D on the basis of their accuracy. Carbon estimates cannot be registered officially unless they are obtained by methods whose accuracy averages at least B. Level B requires modification of look-up tables to specific site conditions; Forest Service regional look-up tables are classified as level C.	For sampling, the standard error cannot exceed 20 percent of the mean estimate.	The sampling error at the 90-percent confidence interval must be <20 percent of the mean estimate. Deductions are applied to the mean carbon estimate if the 90 percent confidence interval is ≥5 percent of the mean.
Exclusions	There is a de minimus provision of up to 3 percent of total emissions.	No de minimus provision.	No de minimus provision.

continued

17

Program	Federal 1605(b) program	California Forestry Sector Protocol, entity reporting	California Forestry Project Protocol, project certification
	Reporting		
Reporting frequency (testing, monitoring, certification)	Annual reporting is required. Reports must be submitted by July 1 for emissions occurring during the previous calendar year.	Registrants must submit annual monitoring reports (Annex C of forestry sector protocol). A complete forest inventory is required every 10 years.	Registrants must submit annual monitoring reports. Third-party certification is required every 5 years. A complete forest inventory is required every 10 years.
	Certification		
Third-party certification	Third-party certification is recommended but not required.	Third-party certification required (biological data must be certified every 5 years). A forest certification protocol is available.	Third-party certification is required. A certification checklist is available (page 69 of the forestry project protocol).
	Forest Activities Accepted		
Forest activities recognized	Reforestation, conservation, and various forest management techniques are eligible for registration under 1605(b).	The program deals with all changes in an entity's carbon stocks.	Forests projects must fall into one of three categories: (1) conservation-based forest management (where management promotes native forests of trees of multiple ages and mixed species), (2) reforestation (of land that has been out of forest cover for a minimum of 10 years), or (3) conservation.
Forest type allowed (native, etc.)	Not specified.	Not specified.	Forest projects must promote native forests.
Required and/or suggested forest management practices	No specific practices are required.	No specific forest practices are required.	See forest activities recognized above.
	Baseline and Additionality		
Additionality	The program does not address this issue.	GHG reductions must follow the forest project protocols, and these address additionality. See forestry project protocol column.	Sequestration gains must be in addition to gains that would have occurred under projected management practices and in addition to what is required by existing law. Calculation of additionality is tied to baseline projections.

continued

Program	Federal 1605(b) program	California Forestry Sector Protocol, entity reporting	California Forestry Project Protocol, project certification
Baseline	A base period of 1 to 4 years is required then reductions are counted against this. Registered reductions can start 2003.	A forecasted baseline is optional, but highly recommended (especially if a project will be done). The forecasted baseline is a projection of an entity's forest carbon stocks over 100 years based on entity's forecasted management practices, starting in 1990 or later (after 2008 the start date must be some subsequent year).	A forecasted baseline required. The forecasted baseline is a projection of an entity's forest carbon stocks based on the entity's forecasted management practices, projected over the project's duration. The projection period may start in 1990 or later (after 2008 the start date must be some subsequent year). Conservation projects must use a baseline based on future land use projections. Reforestation is based on previous practices that have kept the project out of forest cover.
Permanence			
Permanence	There are no permanence requirements.	Permanence is dealt with in the California Forestry Project Protocol.	Forests must be secured with permanent easements.
Crediting period, e.g., length of time carbon credits from registry are valid	The program does address this issue.	The registry does not issue credits.	The registry does not issue credits.
Leakage			
Leakage	Small emitters must certify that none of the reductions reported are likely to cause increases in emissions elsewhere in the entity's operation. Larger emitters must report emissions for the entire entity operation, so leakage is captured.	Onsite leakage analysis and entity level reporting are required for projects being conducted per the forestry project protocol.	An entity must quantify any leakage within the entity's boundaries. It must also assess leakage outside its boundaries and downstream, i.e., indirect effects, as where reforestation uses equipment that uses fossil fuels, but such leakage need not be quantified. Reporting of market leakage is optional but strongly advised and may be required in the future.

Program	Georgia	Maine (in association with Northeast Regional Greenhouse Gas Registry)	Oregon (Department of Forestry)
Governance			
Web site	http://www.gatrees. org/ForestMarketing/ CarbonSequestration.cfm	http://maineghg raabassociates.org/ finalplan.asp http://www.rggr.us/	http://egov.oregon.gov/ODF/ PRIVATE_FORESTS/carbon.shtml
Legal basis	Georgia Carbon Sequestration Registry Act (SB356 2004)	Maine law PL 237 (2003) directs Maine Department of Environmental Protection to create a climate action plan for the State.	Oregon law HB2200 (2001) for forestry offsets

continued

Program	Georgia	Maine (in association with Northeast Regional Greenhouse Gas Registry)	Oregon (Department of Forestry)
Purpose	The law is designed to create an automated, electronic, voluntary registry for offsetting GHG emissions via carbon sequestration and to increase the value of privately owned forests.	The Maine Climate Action Plan proposes measures to cut GHG emissions to 10 percent below 1990 levels by 2020 and mandates an inventory of state-wide emissions and the creation of a GHG registry.	HB2200 authorizes the State forester to aggregate and market carbon offsets from forestry projects on State and private land and calls for creation of a forestry offset accounting system.
Current status	The registry is still under development.	The RGGR is currently in development and should be completed in 2006. The RGGR will not contain specific guidelines for the forestry sector. Instead, the RGGR is to defer to the development of offset protocols by the RGGI, a cooperative agreement by Northeastern and Mid-Atlantic States to reduce GHG emissions. Concurrently, the Forest Service has awarded a grant to the Pinchot Institute to work with Maine, Pennsylvania, and Wisconsin to develop regional protocols, with the intention that these protocols will be applied to State and regional registries in the Northeast.	Development of the registry is more or less on hold until the Oregon Department of Forestry feels there is more market potential for forestry offset projects.
Voluntary or required	Voluntary	The registry is voluntary, but the State is required to complete a GHG inventory.	The program relates to voluntary forestry projects.
Registry management/ State agency responsibilities	A Web-based registration system will be administered by the Georgia Superior Court Clerks' Cooperative Authority. The Georgia Forestry Commission will be responsible for all other aspects of the registry.	The State registry is being developed through a regional effort with NESCAUM. A forestry protocol is in development with Wisconsin and Pennsylvania through a Pinchot Institute research project.	Oregon Department of Forestry is charged with responsibility for developing a forestry accounting system, but this work is currently on hold.
Definition of reporting entity	The reporting entity may be a natural person or a legal entity in its entirety.	This is not yet settled.	The reporting entity must be a non-Federal forest landowner.
Forestry cooperatives recognized	The program is expected to recognize cooperatives of forest landowners.	This is not yet settled. No information available.	This is not yet settled.
Future regulatory promises	Registrants will get a seat at the table in designing any future regulatory program.	This is not yet settled. No information available.	This is not yet settled. No information available.
Compatibility with other carbon programs	Standards have not been established yet, so it is too soon to tell.	Standards are not fully established, but the RGGR will be compatible with the WRI/WBCSD GHG protocol.	Standards are not fully established, but the RGGR will be compatible with the WRI/WBCSD GHG protocol.

continued

Program	Georgia	Maine (in association with Northeast Regional Greenhouse Gas Registry)	Oregon (Department of Forestry)
National and international emissions	Georgia's registry is terrestrial based and will record carbon sequestration. Georgia currently has no statute regulating carbon emissions.	This is not yet settled. No information available.	This is not yet settled. No information available.
Ownership			
Ownership of carbon vs. land ownership	Ownership of carbon is not tied permanently to ownership of land.	This is not yet settled. No information available.	Ownership of carbon can be transferred to those who financed the project. Thus, the Oregon Department of Forestry can obtain rights to carbon credits if the State financed the forest project.
Ownership of dead carbon	Registry will track ownership, but specifics are in development.	This is not yet settled. No information available.	This is not yet settled.
Ownership of live carbon	Registry will track ownership, but specifics are in development.	This is not yet settled. No information available.	This is not yet settled.
Liability			
Liability (who is responsible if project fails to sequester carbon)	Private contracts are expected to regulate this. The registry will record carbon sequestration and expected sequestration. If a project fails to achieve the projected sequestration, the registry will reflect this. However, the registry will not establish contracts regarding carbon trading.	This has not been settled. No information available.	This is not yet settled.
Natural disturbance	See comment above.	This is not yet settled. No information available.	This is not yet settled.
Types of Forest Carbon			
Carbon pools required	Aboveground tree biomass	This is not yet settled. No information available.	This is not yet settled.
Carbon pools voluntary	Soil carbon, belowground live biomass, and forest products.	This is not yet settled. No information available.	This is not yet settled.

continued

Program	Georgia	Maine (in association with Northeast Regional Greenhouse Gas Registry)	Oregon (Department of Forestry)
Offsite carbon			
Wood products	Harvested timber can count as a sink, but details have not yet been arranged.	Specifics are in development. However, recommended guidelines for the Climate Action Plan include use of wood products, and Maine research found sequestration potential in wood-product substitution, e.g., using wood in place of concrete. Future registry development is likely to include provisions for wood products.	HB2200 requires an accounting system to account for emission debits and credits "based on the end product use of harvested biomass." Specifics of wood-product accounting have not been developed yet.
Biomass energy	A policy on biomass energy is in development.	The use of biomass energy to reduce GHGs is encouraged in the Maine Climate Action Plan, but the registry is still in development.	This is not yet established, but the Oregon Department of Forestry is funding research to establish accounting principles for handling forest biofuels as carbon offsets.
	Measurement Methodology		
Calculation/ estimation methods (or metrics and data protocols)	Protocols will include look-up tables for aboveground tree biomass based on specific forest type. Protocols for soils and belowground biomass are in development.	Maine has done a lot of research on forest carbon measurements, but specific registry guidelines have not been developed yet.	This is not yet settled.
Sampling and/or monitoring methods	Specific forest sampling schemes are required based on forest type and age.	Maine has done a lot of research on forest carbon measurements, but specific registry guidelines have not been developed yet.	This is not yet settled.
Accuracy/quality control standards	The program is expected to require third-party certification (with third parties trained by GFC) of all registered carbon sequestration. It is expected that the GFC will monitor 10 percent of areas each year and audit 5 percent of practices each year.	This is not yet settled.	This is not yet settled.
Exclusions	This is not yet settled.	This is not yet settled.	This is not yet settled.
	Reporting		
Reporting frequency (testing, monitoring, and certification)	The statute requires annual reporting.	This is not yet settled.	This is not yet settled.

continued

Program	Georgia	Maine (in association with Northeast Regional Greenhouse Gas Registry)	Oregon (Department of Forestry)
		Certification	
Third-party certification	Third-party certification is required.	This is not yet settled.	The statute encourages third-party certification.
		Forest Activities Accepted	
Forest activities recognized	The program accepts afforestation, reforestation, forest management, and restricted (protected) forests.	Registry guidelines are still in development, but the existing Maine Climate Action Plan proposes many sequestration projects involving forest management techniques in the industrial forest sector.	This is not yet settled, but Oregon is currently funding research on how to include the use of forest biofuels and reduction of fire risk as quantifiable carbon sequestration projects.
Forest type allowed (native, etc.)	Forests must be composed of one or more tree species identified as native to Georgia in Bishop's Native Trees of Georgia.	This is not yet settled.	At present, there is no requirement that forests be composed of native species.
Required and/or suggested forest management practices	Forest activities must meet or exceed Georgia Best Management Practices.	This is not yet settled.	Projects with unsustainable, long-term consequences for the Oregon economy or environment are not accepted, but specifics of this have not been developed yet.
		Baseline and Additionality	
Additionality	There will be two alternative reporting methods for forest management practices, including reforestation. One will consider additionality; the other will not. Carbon will be registered separately for each approach.	This is not yet settled. No information available.	The statute states that offsets will be in addition to those that would result from practices required by the Oregon Forest Practices Act. The State forester must judge that a project "would not occur in the absence of the [offset] agreement."
Baseline	Any year from 1990 on can count as a baseline. Appropriate measurement protocols must be followed for baseline year to qualify.	This is not yet settled. No information available.	This is not yet settled.
		Permanence	
Permanence	Restricted (protected) forest practices will require conservation easements. Other practices will not have easement requirements. A project length will be specified for each project.	This is not yet settled, but permanence requirements of the registry are likely to be accommodating to industrial forests.	This is not yet settled, but the statute states that offsets "account for the duration and permanence of the carbon storage or emission reductions."

continued

Program	Georgia	Maine (in association with Northeast Regional Greenhouse Gas Registry)	Oregon (Department of Forestry)
Crediting period, e.g., length of time carbon credits from registry are valid	This not yet settled, but the statute states that "carbon sequestration results shall reflect the amount of time that net carbon gains are stored." A project length will be specified for each project.	This is not yet settled. No information available.	This is not yet settled, but the statute states that offsets "account for the duration and permanence of the carbon storage or emission reductions."
		Leakage	
Leakage	Leakage will not be considered in afforestation and forest management practices.	This is not yet settled. No information available.	This is not yet settled.

Program	Climate Trust	Chicago Climate Exchange, Commercial Forestry Sector	Chicago Climate Exchange, Exchange Forestry Offsets
		Governance	
Web site	http://www.climatetrust.org	http://www.chicagoclimatex.com/	http://www.chicagoclimatex.com/
Legal basis	Oregon law HB3283 (1997) requires GHG reductions. The CT (a nonprofit organization) is authorized as an offset provider.	The basis is a voluntary, legally binding agreement between interested parties.	The basis is a voluntary, legally binding agreement between interested parties.
Purpose	HB3283 requires new utilities to comply with 0.675 pounds of CO_2 per kilowatt hour GHG performance standard. All utilities have chosen to meet the regulation through carbon offset projects mediated by the nonprofit CT, which issues RFPs for project proposals.	This is a voluntary pilot GHG cap-and-trade program. Participants made a legally binding agreement to reduce emissions to 4 percent below the 1998 to 2001 average by 2006. Under CCX phase II, members are committed to entity-wide emission reductions of 6 percent below baseline by the end of 2010. Commercial forestry sector protocols provide definitions and rules for quantifying and reporting changes in carbon stocks for the commercial forestry sector.	This is a voluntary pilot GHG cap-and-trade program. Participants made a legally binding agreement to reduce emissions to 4 percent below the 1998 to 2001 average by 2006. Under CCX phase II, members are committed to entity-wide emission reductions of 6 percent below baseline by the end of 2010. Offset protocols create criteria for CCX offsets, which members can use to meet GHG reduction requirements.
Current status	The CT is currently implementing projects for utilities within and increasingly outside of the Oregon program. The current offset portfolio includes a number of forestry projects; in order to diversify the portfolio, the CT has set a goal of limiting forestry projects to not more than 25 percent of future offset projects.	Some CCX guidelines are still being developed, but the market is up and running.	Some CCX guidelines are still being developed, but the market is up and running.

continued

Program	Climate Trust	Chicago Climate Exchange, Commercial Forestry Sector	Chicago Climate Exchange, Exchange Forestry Offsets
Voluntary or required	Both mandatory and voluntary participants reduce emissions through the CT's offset portfolio.	This is a voluntary cap-and-trade program; those who join agree to reduce GHG emissions.	This is a voluntary cap-and-trade program; those who join agree to reduce GHG emissions.
Registry management/ State agency responsibilities	The CT funds and reviews offset projects. Projects are evaluated in two phases and then a contract is agreed upon in the third phase.	The CCX has staff and advisors who prepare and administer CCX guidelines.	The CCX has staff and advisors who prepare and administer CCX guidelines.
Definition of reporting entity	Project sponsors submit a project proposal in response to a CT RFP. Accepted projects then become the reporting entities.	Entities can be members (corporations or organizations that directly emit GHGs) or associate members (smaller organizations with little to no direct emissions).	Exchange offsets (of which forestry offsets are one type) are planned reductions in GHG emissions and/or increases in GHG sequestration. These offsets can be registered by CCX members, CCX-registered aggregators, or by CCX project owners if projects meet minimum size requirements.
Forestry cooperatives recognized	Yes	No. The registry deals only with commercial forestry companies.	Forestry cooperatives will be recognized for forestry projects in the future. The CCX currently uses cooperative-type aggregators for farming sequestration projects.
Future regulatory promises	The CT has been cited in many regulatory proceedings and is a member of CCAR. CT offsets may be accredited in future State and/or federally regulated systems.	None	None
Compatibility with other carbon programs	CT has worked with the State of Massachusetts and a utility in Montana to provide offsets. Additionally, Washington has passed legislation compatible with the Oregon law.	The CCX Forest Project rules are consistent with the Kyoto Protocol. The CCX accepts a range of professionally accepted calculation methods.	The CCX Forest Project rules are consistent with the Kyoto Protocol. The CCX accepts a range of professionally accepted calculation methods.
National and international emissions	Projects may be in Oregon, elsewhere in the United States, or outside the United States, with preference given to Oregon projects. International projects usually have a U.S. partner.	The program recognizes emissions and offsets in the United States, Canada, Mexico, and Brazil.	The program recognizes emissions and offsets in the United States, Canada, Mexico, and Brazil.

continued

Program	Climate Trust	Chicago Climate Exchange, Commercial Forestry Sector	Chicago Climate Exchange, Exchange Forestry Offsets
Ownership			
Ownership of carbon vs. land ownership	The CT funds an offset project initially. The carbon stored through the project is then owned by the CT. In the Oregon Power Plant Offset Program, the CT retires the offset credits in perpetuity. In the Large Emitter Program, offsets are transferred to the emitter, who owns them as a corporate asset.	The landowner retains the rights to all nonincluded carbon pools, i.e., branches, roots, litter, and soil.	The landowner retains the rights to all nonincluded carbon pools, i.e., belowground biomass, litter, and soil.
Ownership of dead carbon	NA	Only carbon in the main tree stem is registered with the CCX; the member retains ownership of all remaining carbon (including dead material).	The landowner retains ownership of all nonincluded carbon pools, i.e., belowground biomass, litter, and soil.
Ownership of live carbon	NA	Only carbon in the main tree stem is registered with the CCX; the member retains ownership of all remaining carbon (including dead material).	The landowner retains ownership of all nonincluded carbon pools, i.e., belowground biomass, litter, and soil.
Liability			
Liability (who is responsible if project fails to sequester carbon)	A third party verifies the carbon delivery. Generally if carbon is not delivered, additional funding is stopped and penalties may be assessed.	The program provides for creation of a carbon reserve pool consisting of carbon financial instruments. These instruments are to be released to owners in 2006 if they are not required to cover carbon reductions or losses.	The program provides for creation of a 20-percent reserve pool. The reserves are to be released to owners in 2006 if they are not required to cover carbon reductions or losses.
Natural disturbance	Liability varies depending on specific contracts. Generally, areas affected by natural disturbances that occur in early years must be replanted.	Members must make up for losses due to natural disturbance by surrendering a portion of the reserve pool.	Members must make up for losses due to natural disturbance by surrendering a portion of the reserve pool.
Types of Forest Carbon			
Carbon pools required	This is project specific.	Wood in the main stem of the tree up to the terminal bud	Aboveground living biomass
Carbon pools voluntary	This is project specific.	Carbon in tree roots, leaves, branches, and soil is not counted.	Belowground biomass, litter, and soil carbon may be included in the future

continued

Program	Climate Trust	Chicago Climate Exchange, Commercial Forestry Sector	Chicago Climate Exchange, Exchange Forestry Offsets
Offsite carbon			
Wood products	These may be determined to be eligible in the future, but they are not included at this point.	Not included at this point.	Not included at this point.
Biomass energy	This may be determined to be eligible in the future, but it is not included at this point.	Not included at this point.	Not included at this point.
	Measurement Methodology		
Calculation/ estimation methods (or metrics and data protocols)	These are not specified. Rather, project proposals are evaluated based on their monitoring and verification plan. General guidelines are provided in the 2005 RFP.	The program accepts two general approaches: (1) a carbon-stable accounting approach in which a company certifies that forests are sustainably managed and that carbon stocks will not decrease during the CCX trial period or (2) a model-based accounting approach that employs proprietary timber inventory techniques or publicly available growth-and-yield models.	Participants must use a combination of standard growth coefficients, direct infield sampling, and/or direct measurement performed by independent verifiers. Different methods are required for small, medium, and large forestation projects. The CCX also plans to harmonize offset calculation methods with calculation methods employed in the commercial forestry sector.
Sampling and/or monitoring methods	There are no specific requirements; instead, project proposals are evaluated based on their monitoring and verification plan.	Each entity must have a sampling protocol; there are no other specific requirements as long as overall calculation methods are professionally accepted.	Direct measurement or sampling is required only for large projects (those involving more than 12 500 mt of CO_2 per year).
Accuracy/quality control standards	Third-party verification of measurements made under the monitoring and verification plans is required.	Any carbon estimate models used must be approved by CCX, available for audit, and available to the public to ensure transparency. If a model is used, the member must submit a report detailing the model's quantification methods and procedures. Increases in carbon stocks will be discounted to account for statistical variance associated with the calculation methods used.	All results are subject to inspection.
Exclusions	Information not obtained on this subject for this report.	De minimus exclusions allowed varies by entity size.	Information not obtained on this subject for this report.

continued

Program	Climate Trust	Chicago Climate Exchange, Commercial Forestry Sector	Chicago Climate Exchange, Exchange Forestry Offsets
Reporting			
Reporting frequency (testing, monitoring, and certification)	This is not specified. However, project proposals must outline how and when reporting will occur and CT evaluates this information when considering project proposals. Project-specific monitoring and verification plans are developed with each project. Project implementation must begin within 3 years once funding is awarded.	Annual reporting and an annual audit are required. If the member uses both proprietary timber inventory techniques and publicly available growth-and-yield models, then a report must be provided for each method. An initial report in 2003 and final report at end of the pilot market period are required also.	If an aggregator is involved, each project owner must submit a report to the aggregator, and the aggregator submits a summary report of the whole project to CCX. If there is no aggregator, each project owner or CCX member submits a report to CCX directly. Each project owner must submit an annual attestation that it is in conformance with CCX requirements.
Certification			
Third-party certification	Each project must be certified by a third party that has no financial interest in it.	Changes in carbon stocks must be certified by independent CCX-approved verifiers.	Each project's results must be certified by an independent CCX-approved verifier.
Forest Activities Accepted			
Forest activities recognized	CT recognizes projects in forest preservation, reforestation, afforestation, and forest management practices.	The program is not restricted to a specific forest activity; it applies to any changes in members' forest carbon stocks.	Forest projects can include reforestation and afforestation projects. For certain areas of Brazil and Mexico, projects in avoided deforestation are eligible if there is an accompanying afforestation or reforestation component.
Forest type allowed (native, etc.)	Only native forest projects have been funded.	No specific requirements.	Management of native species is encouraged for sequestration projects.
Required and/or suggested forest management practices	Preference is given to projects with environmental, health, and/or socioeconomic cobenefits.	Members must demonstrate that forest holdings are managed sustainably. CCX accepts standard certification protocols.	Project owners must demonstrate that forest holdings are managed sustainably, and long-term carbon storage must be encouraged. CCX accepts standard certification protocols.
Baseline and Additionality			
Additionality	Offset projects are funded by CT only when sequestration activities would not have occurred in absence of project funding and sequestration gains are above and beyond what is required by law. Projects must not have begun before funding was awarded. Proof of additionality is evaluated by review board on a case-by-case basis.	Additionality is not addressed specifically. No moving baseline is required; a stock exchange approach is employed.	Additionality is not addressed for forestation projects. Avoided deforestation must be in addition to the projected regional preservation trends.

continued

Program	Climate Trust	Chicago Climate Exchange, Commercial Forestry Sector	Chicago Climate Exchange, Exchange Forestry Offsets
Baseline	A "without project" dynamic baseline is required. This baseline projects carbon storage expected in the absence of the project. The project report must describe the assumptions and methods used to create this baseline.	Members must submit initial reports that estimate total carbon stocks on January 1, 2003. These estimates serve as carbon baselines.	Forestation projects must document the carbon stocks present when the projects start. Large forestation projects must quantify baseline levels through direct measurement by a CCX-approved verifier. For avoided deforestation, the regional deforestation rate is used to calculate the baseline—the amount of deforestation that would have occurred without the project.
		Permanence	
Permanence	Project sponsors are required to sign an agreement that ensures delivery of carbon credits in the amount and duration specified in the project proposal. Conservation easements are preferred but permanent easements are not required.	During a pilot marked period, members agree to respect the principle of permanence, excluding catastrophic events and land sales, and to maintain beyond 2006 the quantity of carbon stocks maintained during the pilot period. If land is sold or gained, then members adjust their level of carbon stocks accordingly.	Forest projects must have long-term carbon storage as a primary purpose. Projects qualify if there is a long-term conservation easement, transfer of ownership to a land trust, or under other circumstance the CCZ finds acceptable.
Crediting period, e.g., length of time carbon credits from registry are valid	Project specific	This is not addressed specifically, but the CCX will complete the current GHG reduction round in 2010 (adjusted from original 2006)	This is not addressed specifically, but the CCX will complete the current GHG reduction round in 2010 (adjusted from original 2006).
		Leakage	
Leakage	Proposals must describe how the project will minimize leakage and adjust carbon storage estimates to account for leakage.	Leakage within entity boundaries must be accounted for.	Information not obtained on this subject for this report.

Program	Kyoto Protocol, Clean Development Mechanism	Intergovernmental Panel on Climate Change and Land Use, Land-Use Change and Forestry	World Resources Institute/World Business Council for Sustainable Development Project Protocol
		Governance	
Web site	http://cdm.unfccc.int/	http://unfccc.int/methods_and_science/lulucf/items/1084.php	http://www.ghgprotocol.org/
Legal basis	The basis is an international, legally binding agreement between nations who agreed to sign the protocol.	The basis is a set of voluntary guidelines developed by the IPCC.	The basis is a voluntary protocol for GHG reduction projects developed by the WRI and the WBCSD, two nonprofits.

continued

Program	Kyoto Protocol, Clean Development Mechanism	Intergovernmental Panel on Climate Change and Land Use, Land-Use Change and Forestry	World Resources Institute/ World Business Council for Sustainable Development Project Protocol
Purpose	Annex 1 (developed) countries are to reduce GHG emissions by ~5 percent below 1990 levels by 2008–12. Annex 1 countries can offset 1 percent of their base-year emissions through sequestration activities (authorized through CDMs). Also, a CDM registry is to be developed and maintained and publicly available database of CDM projects is to be created.	To establish "good practice guidance" for estimating carbon emissions and sequestration for land use, land use change, and forestry activities. The program is designed for creating national GHG inventories and does not establish a registry.	To establish internationally accepted accounting and reporting standards for GHG emission reduction or sequestration projects. The Project Protocol follows the WRI/WBCSD GHG Protocol, which created standards for emission reporting.
Current status	The CDM registration process is up and running but no forestry projects have been approved as of October 2005, and no forestry methodologies have been approved by executive board.	LULUCF guidelines were issued in 2003.	The Project Protocol was made public in December 2005; sector-specific protocols (which will include a protocol for the forestry sector) will be issued in 2006.
Voluntary or required	It is a cap-and-trade program.	Voluntary	Voluntary
Registry management/ State agency responsibilities	The CDM Executive Board is the official administrative body. Members are elected every 2 years by the Kyoto Conference of the Parties.	Guidelines are issued by the IPCC and interested parties can follow them if they wish.	Guidelines are issued by the WRI/ WBCSD and interested parties can follow them if they wish.
Definition of reporting entity	The program is applied on a project basis. A "project" is a planned set of activities for reducing carbon emissions through afforestation or reforestation. CDMs must take place in nonannex 1 countries that are parties to the Kyoto protocol. A "purchasing" country must have a national GHG inventory in place.	NA	A project is any activity or group of activities designed to reduce GHG emission levels or increase GHG removal from the atmosphere, e.g., through terrestrial sequestration. An entity that wants to quantify GHG reductions at the corporate or entity-wide level should use the WRI/WBCSD Corporate Accounting Standard.
Forestry cooperatives recognized?	Not yet specified	NA	The program has not addressed this question. The question may not be addressed until land use sector protocols are developed.
Future regulatory promises	If approved, a CDM counts as an offset to GHG emissions for the annex 1 country or company that financed the CDM.	NA	NA

continued

Program	Kyoto Protocol, Clean Development Mechanism	Intergovernmental Panel on Climate Change and Land Use, Land-Use Change and Forestry	World Resources Institute/World Business Council for Sustainable Development Project Protocol
Compatibility with other carbon programs	CDM must be located in developing countries, so direct compatibility with U.S. registries isn't possible. However, guidelines for CDM forest methodologies (when these are fully developed) will likely be stricter than those for any other registry.	LULUCF is widely recognized but it may be too general to transfer to actual carbon registries. This subject requires further investigation not covered in this report.	The program meets Kyoto CDM requirements in principle (the Project Protocol Web site compares key concepts of both systems).
National and international emissions	Sequestration projects must occur in developing countries participating in the Kyoto Protocol.	Inventory methods would be applicable to both.	The program is an international accord and works with both national and international projects.
Ownership			
Ownership of carbon vs. land ownership	Carbon ownership moves with CDM projects.	NA	NA
Ownership of dead carbon	The program does not deal with wood products.	NA	NA
Ownership of live carbon	Live carbon belongs to the project host until the CDM is registered and purchased by an annex I entity.	NA	NA
Liability			
Liability (who is responsible if project fails to sequester carbon)	Information not obtained on this subject for this report.	The program does not deal with project level reporting.	Information not obtained on this subject for this report.
Natural disturbance	No specific forest methodologies have been adopted yet.	Information not obtained on this subject for this report.	Information not obtained on this subject for this report.
Types of Forest Carbon			
Carbon pools required	If a project shows that certain carbon pools will not contribute to increased emissions, then these pools need not be measured. All other carbon pools must be measured.	Aboveground living biomass and organic soil are required for all tiers. For tiers 2 and 3, belowground biomass, dead woody biomass, litter, and mineral soil must be calculated also.	The program has not addressed this point specifically; the point will be discussed in the 2006 land use sector protocols.

continued

Program	Kyoto Protocol, Clean Development Mechanism	Intergovernmental Panel on Climate Change and Land Use, Land-Use Change and Forestry	World Resources Institute/World Business Council for Sustainable Development Project Protocol
Carbon pools voluntary	Those that will not contribute significantly to increases in emissions may be reported. (Unable to find for this report the specific numbers for what counts as a significant emission.)	For tier 1, voluntary pools are belowground biomass, dead woody biomass, litter, and mineral soil (unless the land in question was previously unforested, in which case calculation of mineral soil carbon is required).	The program has not addressed this point specifically; the point will be discussed in the 2006 land use sector protocols.
Offsite carbon			
Wood products	Not accepted	Wood products are assumed to oxidize completely when harvested. However, if it can be shown that stocks of wood products are increasing, there is flexibility in the reporting mechanism.	The program has not addressed this point specifically but may do so in the 2006 land use sector protocols.
Biomass energy	Not accepted	Not addressed	The program has not addressed this point specifically but may do so in the 2006 land use sector protocols.
	Measurement Methodology		
Calculation/ estimation methods (or metrics and data protocols)	These must be approved by the executive board. No forestry methods have been approved yet.	Two approaches are described: (1) calculation of annual change in carbon stocks resulting from annual losses and gains in carbon stocks and (2) a stock exchange method in which carbon inventories are taken at two points in time and then compared.	Project developers must describe the methods to be employed—that is, whether direct measurement, models, or other techniques will be used. The Project Protocol provides formulas for calculating biological sequestration.
Sampling and/or monitoring methods	These must be approved by the executive board. No forestry methods have been approved yet.	Information not obtained on this subject for this report.	Project developers must develop a monitoring plan for all identified primary and secondary GHG effects of the project.
Accuracy/quality control standards	Methodologies (and corresponding quality control) must be approved by executive board.	Three tiers of data standards are employed depending on the importance of the carbon pool to the overall carbon budget and the country-specific data available. Tier 1 uses default LULUCF values; higher tiers are asked to report sources of all emission and sequestration data, results of any models used, and analysis of emission changes.	They must describe how they will store data and establish quality assurance/quality control and must state the uncertainty involved in their measurement and/or estimation tools.
Exclusions	Information not obtained on this subject for this report.	Information not obtained on this subject for this report.	None listed
	Reporting		
Reporting frequency (testing, monitoring, and certification)	Information not obtained on this subject for this report.	Information not obtained on this subject for this report	None listed.

continued

Program	Kyoto Protocol, Clean Development Mechanism	Intergovernmental Panel on Climate Change and Land Use, Land-Use Change and Forestry	World Resources Institute/World Business Council for Sustainable Development Project Protocol
Certification			
Third-party certification	Project design must be validated by a "designated operational entity" prior to registration (requires a 45-day notice and comment period). The CDM Executive Board must certify project. Emission reductions must be verified by the operational entity.	This is not explicitly required. Section 5.7.3 offers several "good practice" recommendations for verifying results.	The program does not address this issue. Transparency and reporting standards are provided, but the program does not offer guidance on how to solicit or conduct third-party certification.
Forest Activities Accepted			
Forest activities recognized	The program recognizes only reforestation and afforestation projects. Reforestation must be on land degraded or unforested since 1989.	Because the program has to do with changes in overall carbon stocks of individual nations, changes in stocks are recorded regardless of the type of forest activity.	The program has not addressed this point specifically but may do so in the 2006 land use sector protocols.
Forest type allowed (native, etc.)	Projects must monitor and remedy any negative environmental or socioeconomic impact, but the issue of native forests is not addressed directly.	There are no forest type requirements; the guidelines are for an inventory of all carbon stocks, regardless of species.	The program has not addressed this point specifically but may do so in the 2006 land use sector protocols.
Required and/or suggested forest management practices	Any negative socioeconomic or environmental impact must be monitored and remedied according to native country's law.	Information not obtained on this subject for this report.	The program has not addressed this point specifically but may do so in the 2006 land use sector protocols.
Baseline and Additionality			
Additionality	Carbon sequestration must be in addition to sequestration that would have occurred without the project.	The inventory doesn't deal with reductions at the individual-project level, which is the level at which additionality is considered.	This is addressed only indirectly, through the baseline requirements.

continued

Program	Kyoto Protocol, Clean Development Mechanism	Intergovernmental Panel on Climate Change and Land Use, Land-Use Change and Forestry	World Resources Institute/World Business Council for Sustainable Development Project Protocol
Baseline	The baseline must project how carbon pools would change over time if the project were not implemented. Three baseline approaches are specified. Projects must begin after 2001.	Simple stock change or annual increment can be used since this is an inventory approach.	The program provides details for (1) a performance standard procedure and (2) a project-specific baseline procedure. Both procedures involve identifying a baseline scenario which "describes an activity or a set of activities that result in GHG emissions against which project activity emissions can be compared." A project developer must describe the estimation and measurement techniques used to establish baseline emission levels.
Permanence			
Permanence	The CDM allows projects to generate credits for up to 60 years, subject to verification every 5 years. It allows temporary CERs (10-year max) and long-term CERs (up to 60 years).	The program simply tracks carbon stocks over time and does not address permanence.	The program does not deal with permanence; this is left to discretion of project developer.
Crediting period, e.g., length of time carbon credits from registry are valid	This is either a maximum of 20 years with two renewals possible (60 years total) or a maximum of 30 years with no renewal.	The program does not issue credits.	The program does not issue credits.
Leakage			
Leakage	Leakage is defined as an increase in GHG emissions outside the project boundary that is attributable to a CDM project. Projects must be designed to minimize leakage and must monitor for leakage.	Information not obtained on this subject for this report. However, leakage doesn't seem applicable as LULUCF deals more with national level GHG inventories.	Leakage is discussed as "secondary effects." Project developers are asked to define primary and secondary effects of the GHG reduction project and consider all secondary effects that are significant in quantifying GHG reductions.

DOE = U.S. Department of Energy; GHG = greenhouse gas; CCX = Chicago Climate Exchange; CDM = Clean Development Mechanism; NA = not applicable; FPP = forestry project protocol; COLE = carbon online estimator; RGGR = Regional Greenhouse Gas Registry; RGGI = Regional Greenhouse Gas Initiative; NESCAUM = Northeast States for Coordinated Air Use Management; WRI = World Resources Institute; WBCSD = World Business Council for Sustainable Development; GFC = Georgia Forestry Commission; CT = Climate Trust; RFP = request for proposals; CCAR = CA Climate Action Registry; IPCC = Intergovernmental Panel on Climate Change; LULUCF = land use, land-use change and forestry; CER = certified emission reduction. This comparison of carbon registries, forestry sector, includes registries and other related protocols.

Appendix B
Forest Carbon Definitions

Additionality: emission reduction or sequestration that is in addition to reduction or sequestration that would occur in a "business as usual" scenario. For example, if State law requires a forestland owner to replant an area with trees, then carbon sequestered through the planting is not additional, since the landowner was legally required to plant it.

Afforestation: the process of replanting and/or growing forests on land that has not been forested in recent history.

Allowances: often refers to the basic tradable commodity within greenhouse gas emission trading systems. Allowances grant their holder the right to emit a specific quantity of pollution once, e.g., 1 ton of carbon dioxide.

Baseline: a point in time, or a level of carbon, from which an entity or project will measure changes in carbon stocks.

Biological emissions: greenhouse gas (GHG) emissions that are released directly to the atmosphere from biomass, both live and dead. For forests, biological emissions are GHG emissions released from forest biomass, both live and dead, including forest soils.

Carbon dioxide equivalent: the unit of measurement used to indicate the global warming potential of greenhouse gases. It is used to evaluate the impacts of releasing (or avoiding the release of) different greenhouse gases.

Carbon sequestration: the removal of carbon from the atmosphere.

Carbon sink: a reservoir or depository that can absorb carbon dioxide from the atmosphere. Forests are a common form of sink.

Credit: carbon sequestered in excess of the required amount.

Downstream effects: secondary greenhouse gas effects associated with the products produced by a project activity.

Entity: the unit that participates in a registry—commonly a corporation, city, county, or State government, or other legally constituted body.

Forest carbon sequestration: can occur through afforestation, reforestation, and alteration of land management practices to maximize carbon retention on the land. Forest carbon can be sequestered in aboveground biomass, roots, soils, woody debris, and postharvest wood products.

Geological carbon sequestration: the removal of carbon from the atmosphere by injecting carbon dioxide directly into underground geological formations.

Global warming potential: a term used to describe the relative potency, molecule for molecule, of a greenhouse gas (GHG), taking into account how long it remains active in the atmosphere. The global warming potentials (GWP) currently used are those calculated over 100 years. Carbon dioxide is taken as the gas of reference, with a 100-year GWP of 1. All the other GHGs have a much higher GWP than carbon dioxide, molecule for molecule. Carbon dioxide still has a higher net impact on global warming, though, because it is present at much higher concentrations in the atmosphere than are the other GHGs.

Gas	Global warming potential (approximate)	Concentration in atmosphere (ppbv)
Carbon dioxide (CO_2)	1	358,000
Methane (CH_4)	21	1,721
Nitrous oxide (N_2O)	310	311
Hydrofluorocarbons (HFCs) (HCFC–22 as an example)	1,300 – 1,400	0.105
Perfluorocarbons (PFCs) (CF_4 as an example)	6,500	0.070
Hexafluoride (SF_6)	23,900	0.032

ppbv = Concentrations expressed as "parts per billion volume." Concentrations listed are for 1994 atmospheric levels.

Greenhouse gas: the term greenhouse gas (GHG) refers to a set of gases that all add heat to the Earth's atmosphere, namely carbon dioxide, methane, nitrous oxide, hydrofluorocarbons, perfluorocarbons, and sulfur hexafluoride. GHGs accomplish a warming effect because they all absorb and emit radiation at specific wavelengths within the spectrum of infrared radiation emitted by the Earth's surface, the atmosphere, and the clouds. The radiation emitted by the GHGs increases the temperature of the Earth's atmosphere.

Leakage: the extent to which events occurring outside the project boundary tend to reduce a project's carbon dioxide emissions benefit. For example, avoiding deforestation in one place might lead to acceleration of deforestation in some other place. This can apply to all types of carbon dioxide reduction projects.

Nonbiological emissions: greenhouse gas (GHG) emissions that are not directly released from biomass. For example, GHGs from fossil fuel combustion qualify as nonbiological emissions.

Offset: the results of an action implemented to avoid, sequester, or displace emissions of carbon dioxide. Offsets are often referred to in the context of a regulatory scheme—occurring when there is a surplus created by voluntary reductions in excess of required reductions. Offsets can become credits, which can be traded, in a cap-and-trade regulatory system.

Permanence: ability of a project to weather exposure to variables and events that put at risk its ability to maintain the reduction in carbon dioxide output. Permanent projects permanently avoid or displace emissions of carbon dioxide; nonpermanent projects offer the reduction in carbon dioxide output only for a limited amount of time.

Project: a planned activity or set of activities to remove, reduce, or prevent carbon dioxide emissions in the atmosphere.

Reforestation: replanting trees in recently harvested areas.

Registry: legal way for entities to list sequestered carbon. Registries vary in scope, inclusions, verifiability, and protocols.

Reservoir: area where carbon is stored.

Sink: the process, activity, or mechanism that removes carbon from the atmosphere by absorbing and storing it, thereby offsetting carbon dioxide emissions.

Terrestrial carbon sequestration: the removal of carbon from the atmosphere through fixation of carbon dioxide by terrestrial vegetation. All vegetation types sequester some carbon—rangeland, row crops, wetlands, forests, etc. The rate of sequestration, however, varies by vegetation type.

Upstream effects: secondary greenhouse gas effects of a project's activities associated with their input. For example, an afforestation project involves activities such as growing and transporting the nursery stock. These activities can have upstream effects (or externalities that have not been internalized) in terms of fossil fuel consumption or pesticide and fertilizer use.